SEIZED BY SHADOWS

THE ART OF BEING SEIZED

K.C.PRAKALYA

Contents

Acknowledgements — v

1. HEAVEN'S BRUSHSTROKES ON EARTH — 1

2. DANCING WITH DOUBT — 3

3. THE DUALITY WITHIN — 4

4. INKSTORM OF FEELINGS — 5

5. LIFE'S FRAGRANT DICHOTOMY — 6

6. PETALS PONDERING PASSION — 8

7. HEARTWOOD CONFESSIONS — 9

8. A FRACTURED CONNECTION — 11

9. NATURE'S LAMENT — 12

10. NATURE'S FESTIVE INVITATION — 13

11. LOVE UNSPOKEN — 14

12. THE ANATOMY OF LOVE — 15

13. WHISPERS OF AN ABSENT HEART — 16

14. SWEET WHISPERS OF LOVE — 17

15. HEARTSTRINGS THROUGH THE SEASONS — 18

16. FRAGMENTS OF A FORGOTTEN ROMANCE — 19

17. ALCHEMY OF HEARTS — 20

18. SPARK OF LASTING LOVE — 21

19. NAVIGATING THE IMPERFECT — 22

20. THE APPETITE OF TIME — 23

21. A SOUL'S JOURNEY — 25

22. VEINS OF SENTIMENT — 26

23. ENERGY UNLEASHED — 27

24. CHAINS OF WRATH — 28

25. A SILENT FIRE — 29

26. BEAUTY IN DESTRUCTION — 30

27. THE SYMPHONY OF SOLACE — 31

Contents

28. RAGING RIVERS AND GENTLE BREEZES 32

29. STILLNESS AMONG THE STORM 33

30. THE UNMOVED ECHO 35

31. THE SILENT WITNESS 36

32. VEILS OF SILENCE UNRAVELED 37

33. SERENITY IN FLUX 38

34. BUILD OR BANISH 39

35. VERSES IN TWO TONES 40

36. WOVEN IN WORDINGS 41

37. THE HIDDEN ESSENCE 42

38. TO THAT ONE WOMAN 43

39. THE NATURE OF NURTURE 44

40. THE LIGHTHOUSE OF HER LOVE 45

41. A MATERNAL MELODY 46

42. SYMBOLS IN THE SORROW 47

43. CHAINS OF THE DOMESTIC DREAM 48

44. TATTERED WINGS OF GRACE 50

45. RED THREADS OF CONQUEST 51

46. THE COLOURS OF RESILIENCE 53

47. THE BEHOLDER'S LENS 55

48. SHADOWS IN THE SPOTLIGHT 57

49. THE ART OF FACADES 58

50. A LOVE LETTER TO MY MOTHER INDIA 59

Acknowledgements

As I take this moment to reflect on the journey of publishing my poetry book, I feel it is essential to acknowledge the incredible support I have received from those around me.

First and foremost, I would like to extend my heartfelt gratitude to my professors. Your guidance, encouragement, and constructive feedback have been invaluable in honing my craft and inspiring my creativity. Your passion for literature and unwavering belief in my potential have truly made a lasting impact on my journey as a poet.

Then to my parents, thank you for your endless love and support. You have always encouraged me to express myself and pursue my passion for poetry, and for that, I am eternally grateful.

Lastly, to my friends, your companionship and motivation have meant the world to me. I am incredibly grateful for your support and encouragement throughout this process.

Also, I would like to express my heartfelt gratitude to dear Veena for her invaluable assistance in proofreading my poetry book. Your keen eye for detail and insightful feedback were instrumental in refining my work, and I truly appreciate the time and effort you dedicated to this project. Your support not only helped enhance the quality of my writing but also boosted my confidence as a poet. I am grateful to have someone as talented and dedicated as you in my corner. Thank you once again for your generosity and expertise.

I want to take a moment to extend my heartfelt gratitude to P. Dhanushkumar, my best friend, for your incredible work on the cover page of my poetry book and for your skillful editing throughout the writing process. Your creative vision truly brought my words to life, and the cover design perfectly encapsulates the essence of my poetry. I appreciate the countless hours you dedicated to ensuring that every detail was just right. Thank you once again for your invaluable contributions. I could not have done this without your support and talent.

1. HEAVEN'S BRUSHSTROKES ON EARTH

As water that contains multiple colours;
As a weaver bird, which cleverly builds
It's nest by using its tiny beak;
As a baby inside mother's womb
Turns into a gigantic creature
With minute functional system and organs
Making us remember his presence.

2. DANCING WITH DOUBT

3. THE DUALITY WITHIN

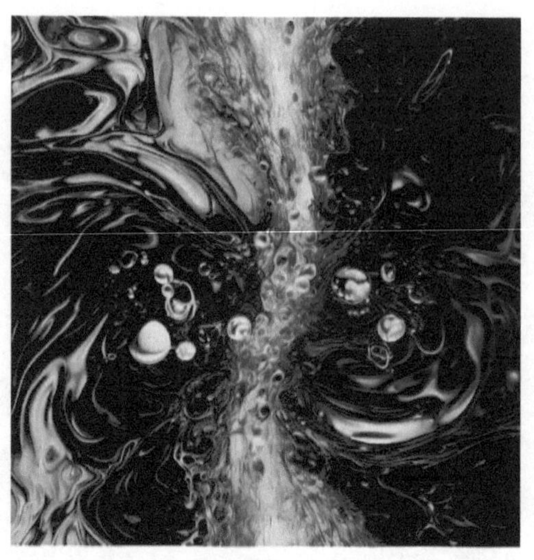

Not every drop of mine is pure,
But still, I'm valuable
People search me for their cure;
Sometimes I become contagious,
But still, I'm valuable
Some feel prestigious
Because of me;
I'm colourful as well as
I'm colourless;
I give pain as well as
I give life.

4. INKSTORM OF FEELINGS

They use every drop my mine

To get lost in fantasy;

To attain peace;

To show their power;

To register everything legally;

Till the last drop of mine.

Then they throw me like a used tissue

As if I'm useless…

5. LIFE'S FRAGRANT DICHOTOMY

How amazing are roses,
When my life freezes.
Standing at the down,
Makes me mourn.
How amazing are roses,
When my life freezes.
Thinking of the Rose's thorns,
Which immediately forewarns
The dual nature of life.

K.C.PRAKALYA

How amazing are roses,
When my life freezes.

6. PETALS PONDERING PASSION

I'm soft, gentle, and pure
One of my petals wishes to cure;
I need not to be a garland
I need not to be a perfume
Or in a funeral procession.
Rather, I wish to be
At the feet of the Lord
As an honour for his creation.

7. HEARTWOOD CONFESSIONS

I plead you not as a source of your life,
But as a creature
Which longs for love.

8. A FRACTURED CONNECTION

9. NATURE'S LAMENT

When I was small
The trees were around me.
They guided me
Wherever I go.
But now,
The buildings are around me
Where I search for the key.

10. NATURE'S FESTIVE INVITATION

I'm invited
Where the moon is laughing,
The stars are dancing,
The clouds are clashing,
To aglow the venue
By lightning and thunder
As the party begins,
Nature welcomes me.

11. LOVE UNSPOKEN

12. THE ANATOMY OF LOVE

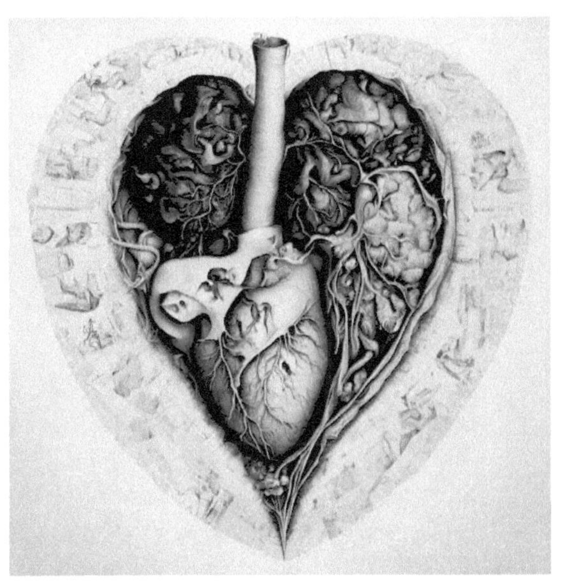

13. WHISPERS OF AN ABSENT HEART

My eyes longs for your eyes on me
My ears crave to hear your voice
My heart wishes you to heal
In order to receive some zeal,
Oh, my soul!
Oh, my soul!

14. SWEET WHISPERS OF LOVE

The colours of the rainbow,
Seems to fade away.
The hues of the morning mist
Seems to be dull and
Less impressive.
The buzzing of the bees,
That makes me to think
The conversations we had
Oh! How sweet as the nectar.

15. HEARTSTRINGS THROUGH THE SEASONS

That lightning and thunder
Remembers the day
I fell in love with you.
The drop of rain that landed on me,
Remembers your kissing.
The rain's scent,
Brings back your pheromones.
The drop of rain that seeped into my skin
Remembers how your touch felt.

16. FRAGMENTS OF A FORGOTTEN ROMANCE

The frozen moon in the sky
It caused me to fondly recall you
The cold blood that rushes high
And how the agony kills me
As a bird tries in the cage to flee;
Like the sun waiting for the morning,
One day I will wait for an adorning.

17. ALCHEMY OF HEARTS

My heart beats
As cold as the breeze,
As soon as I met you,
It left me a cue
I met my soulmate!
And you will remain as my comate.

18. SPARK OF LASTING LOVE

Our eyes were overflowing
With tears,
At the beginning of our journey.
Our eyes were overflowing
With tears,
As we prepared to conclude.
But the real love we shared
Brought us together.

19. NAVIGATING THE IMPERFECT

20. THE APPETITE OF TIME

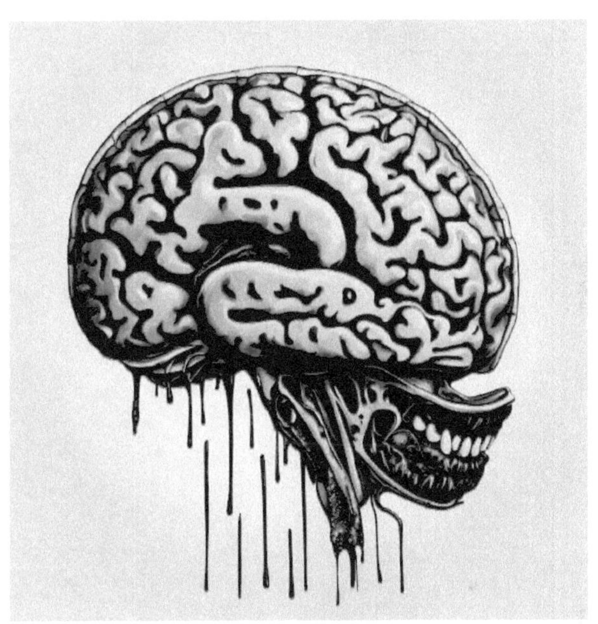

Oh! My brain
Constantly eating;
Not the food we eat
But,
The memories.
Oh! Crafty brain
You are so genius

That you eat only
The digested memories;
That's how some memories
Fade away.

21. A SOUL'S JOURNEY

I went on a journey,
Which was a canny
As well as unpalatable.
I thought of eradicable
The unpalatable one,
The solutions were none.
Which gave me a lesson
That it is impossible to lessen
The bad and receive only the good,
That everyone could.

22. VEINS OF SENTIMENT

Not only it pumps blood,
Also, the emotion
That goes hand in hand with motion,
Like the heart's Love,
Mind's Envy, and
The most important, Happiness!

23. ENERGY UNLEASHED

Anybody can become angry,
It will come in a hurry.
Are you showing your anger
To the right person?
At the right time?
For the right purpose?
Think…

24. CHAINS OF WRATH

I threw a stone

Which has gone,

Deep inside a sea

And makes me

To comprehend that

The same goes for the words.

25. A SILENT FIRE

In a flash of lightning,
Mind goes for a driving
Heart performs a swinging
Tone started rising
Makes realising
As well as reminding.

26. BEAUTY IN DESTRUCTION

Feeling sad,
Sometimes being mad
Still, the impact lasts in me
As I was lost in the deep sea
Caught in a black hole
Which swallows me as a whole.

27. THE SYMPHONY OF SOLACE

28. RAGING RIVERS AND GENTLE BREEZES

As I step outside,
There were no feelings from inside.
The flames were fuming in me
Like waves that are outraged by the sea,
Silence was surrounded everywhere
As if the earth didn't exist,
Except the cold breeze that kissed me
To help me relax and be free.

29. STILLNESS AMONG THE STORM

Some paths can be longer

Some paths can be shorter

Generations may change

And the places can range,

People can go from

One country to another;

Their language may change

Their feelings can range
But silence remains the same.

30. THE UNMOVED ECHO

It can be in the harsh cry
Also, in one's own shy;
It can be in the cutest smile
Also, when emotions are at a pile;
It can be in the saddest moan
When someone has gone.

31. THE SILENT WITNESS

There lies a thing
In the crashing waves;
There lies a thing
In the cacophony of sounds from wildlife;
There lies a thing
Even in a rushing rain.

32. VEILS OF SILENCE UNRAVELED

33. SERENITY IN FLUX

Can feel something
On the shore, keenly listening
To the crashing waves in the sea,
Can feel something
In the refreshing darkness,
Singing alone with the nightingale,
Can feel something…

34. BUILD OR BANISH

Words have the ability
To both create and destroy
In relationships,
Words are really important
Because, those three words
Have the power to start
And end a relationship.

35. VERSES IN TWO TONES

It can captivate you,
Which can easily glue
To someone or something.
It can give pain to you
Which one cannot chew;
It can provide happiness
As well as sadness;
It can bring glory
Also, it has the ability
To create a huge story.

36. WOVEN IN WORDINGS

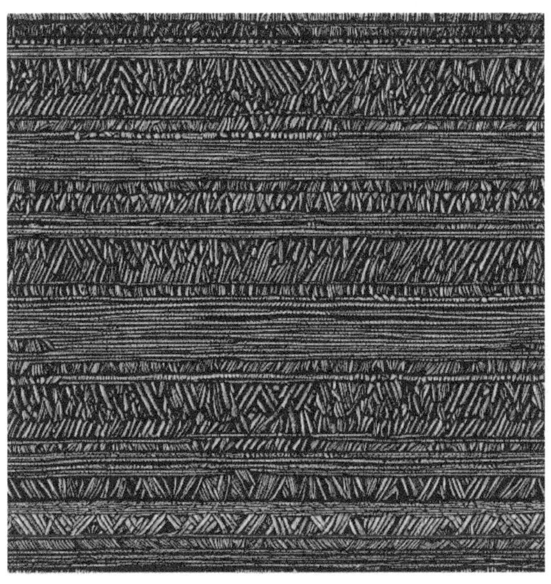

Words, words, words,
Fly like birds;
Words, words, words,
Do have records;
It doesn't matter
Whether it's longer
Or being shorter
Words, words, words,
Carry meaning in herds.

37. THE HIDDEN ESSENCE

I have

Hippopotomonstrosesquippedaliophobia

I hate them

Because, I love

Being short and crisp;

I too know to twist

With palindrome

Playing in Rome

Just to go hand in hand

With Horace's command.

38. TO THAT ONE WOMAN

Where did you get that energy?
To be a teacher;
To be a chef;
To be a friend;
To be a caretaker;
Despite of having a busy schedule,
You were with me entirely.

39. THE NATURE OF NURTURE

40. THE LIGHTHOUSE OF HER LOVE

A mother is the goddess of seeing eye
Who even transforms,
Her blood into milk
For her infant to consume.
Every woman should feel proud
To achieve the most
Precious stage of motherhood
As reincarnation.

41. A MATERNAL MELODY

The love that you have is priceless
Which appears to be voiceless;
But it has multiple layers
That reflects in your daily prayers
Whenever I need a hug,
You'll always have your hands open;
Whenever I feel depressed
You made me feel so blessed.

42. SYMBOLS IN THE SORROW

43. CHAINS OF THE DOMESTIC DREAM

Why does she lose her wings?
Why does she wander lonely as a deserted ship?
Because,
She is SHE.

44. TATTERED WINGS OF GRACE

45. RED THREADS OF CONQUEST

As an angel
And after that
There will be no one
For SHE.

46. THE COLOURS OF RESILIENCE

I'm here for a purpose,
To achieve something
To live my life
To enjoy my freedom
To experience happiness.
I'm not here,
Only for you,

To satisfy your physical pleasures
To be your slave
To be in the closed doors.
Rather,
I'm here for a purpose
And I'm not an object.

47. THE BEHOLDER'S LENS

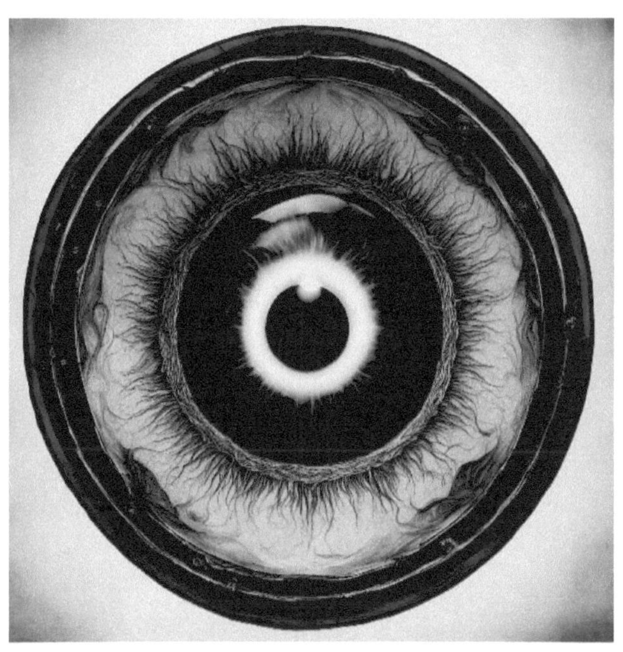

It may be
Beautiful or ugly;
She may be
Fair or dark;
He may be
Slim or fat;
They may be

Tall or short;
And everything
Lies in the eyes.

48. SHADOWS IN THE SPOTLIGHT

In the entire earth,
The seeds of evil were sown
Which gave birth to the
Multiple entities are grown.
They have the cutest smile
With the deep inside guile.

49. THE ART OF FACADES

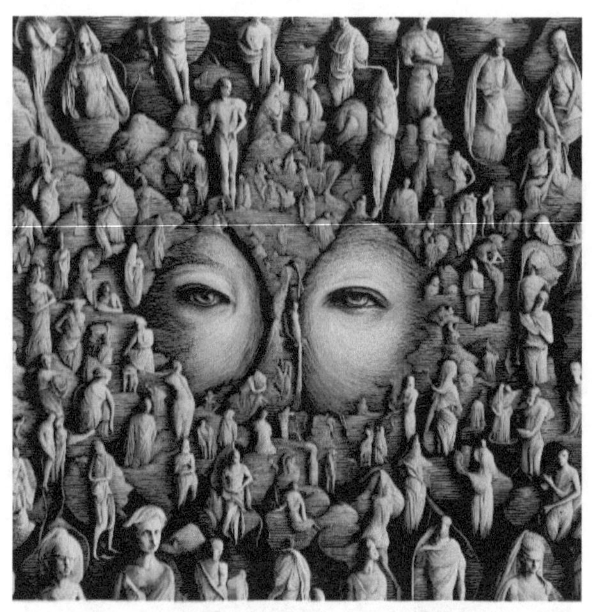

We cross many people,
In our lives;
Who wanders around us
With different shades of
Faces wearing masks,
Changing whenever they want
With which they haunt.

50. A LOVE LETTER TO MY MOTHER INDIA

India is my motherland,
For her children, she became a brand.
She is the seventh largest country by land
Mountains, Rivers, Hills, Oceans make her grand.
She is beautiful and rich in culture,
Representing her motherhood by nurture.
Having deeply rooted through her scriptures
She is gorgeously positioned in her sculptures.

I love my mother, India.
Who wears a chain of mountains like Vindhya;
She is known for her Unity in Diversity
Her constitution gains respect through authenticity.
I tells her Independent nature;
N tells her Name, which is beyond the cloud;
D tells her world's largest Democracy;
I tells her Indian Ocean, home to thousands of islands;
A tells her Awesomeness in everything.
We hold her flag in special occurrence,
Which turns us to be her patrons.
Her flag comprises Saffron, White and Green
More significance the colours mean.

9 798889 556589